The Shit Book

The Shit Book

The Poop Book

Thomas N. Bainter

Order this book online at www.trafford.com
or email orders@trafford.com

Most Trafford titles are also available at major online book retailers.

Printed in the United States of America.

ISBN: 978-1-4669-0363-0 (sc)
ISBN: 978-1-4669-0365-4 (hc)
ISBN: 978-1-4669-0364-7 (e)

Library of Congress Control Number: 2011919760

Trafford rev. 11/02/2011

 www.trafford.com

North America & international
toll-free: 1 888 232 4444 (USA & Canada)
phone: 250 383 6864 ♦ fax: 812 355 4082

This book is about shit. Not the shit you have in your closet or laying around the house or the shit in your car, it is about shit. The stuff that comes out of your body when you have to go to the bathroom. Not the stuff that comes out the front side but the stuff that comes out of your butt. It doesn't matter how poor you are, how rich you are, how ugly you are or how beautiful you are. It doesn't matter if you are skinny or over weight. And no matter what you may think, your shit does stink sometimes. This book is for all of you who have ever admired your dirty deed. For those of you whose brother made you run to the bathroom because you thought someone had died only to see the longest turd ever in the stool.

The Bulimia Shit:

The one where when you have diarrhea so bad it makes you throw up your food.

The Lincoln Log Shit:

Anyone older than 40 can picture this without a picture.

The Hershey Squirts Shit:

When it feels like your butt is a squeezable ketchup bottle.

The Spaghetti Shit:

Long skinny stings.

The Snake Shit:

Of course there is no need for a picture as the name implies the vision.

The Mile Long Shit also known as the Roger Bannister Shit:

It is so long that you wonder if it is out in the street and you are only seeing the top five feet of it.

The Gomer Pyle Shit:

More like a dog pile but bigger.

The Ice Cream Cone Shit:

Once again the picture isn't needed to visualize.

The Creamed Corn Shit:

We all have this one from time to time after eating 10 ears of sweet corn.

The Golden Nugget Shit:

Kind of similar to the creamed corn shit but this one just has some golden nuggets incased by black debris.

The Baby Slime Shit:

Comes from a baby but you are not sure if they just put it in their mouth or it just came out.

The Texas Chili Shit:

The one where you understand what the real purpose of snow cones are.

The Explosive Diarrhea Shit:

We all have had these, happy to have made it to the toilet (if we did). When the joint chief of staff come knocking at your door wanting you to help them with their latest war as a secret weapon.

The Curly Sue Shit:

This can happen with any number of the above shits and looks so cute at the top.

The Time of the Month Shit:

When there is some red stuff mixed in and you aren't sure if you should call your doctor.

The Titanic Shit:

It starts as a floater but then it sinks.

The Floater Shit:

You aren't sure if they will ever flush down.

The Plumber Shit:

When you need to get a plumber to get rid of it.

The Bread Loaf Shit:

When you are out in the woods and drop trou and pinch off a loaf.

The Broken Hearted Shit:
(AKA the bathroom stall shit)

Where you sit all broken hearted cause you came to shit but only farted.

The Rainbow Shit:

Where there are so many different colors you try to remember what you ate the past couple of days.

The King Kong Shit:

Shit so massive you have no idea how you were able to push it out.

The Lamaze Class Shit:

Where you were so happy you went to Lamaze class with your wife to learn breathing techniques so you could get your "proud baby" out.

The Train Shit:

Where there is a bunch of connecting pieces.

The out of Order Shit:

When it stinks so bad people have to walk 200 feet from the door.

The Funeral Home Shit:

When you walk into a bathroom and it smells like somebody just died.

The Seafood Shit:

When you can see some of the stuff you just ate.

The Telephone Book Shit:

Where you grab the telephone book to find somebody to call so they can come over and see your masterpiece.

The Caddy Shack Shit:

Where it looks like a Baby Ruth at the bottom of the pool.

The War and Peace Shit:

Where it takes so long you could have wrote a novel.

The Saving Private Ryan Shit:

Where if it was up to you to save him you wouldn't have been able to do it because after you got off the toilet, you couldn't walk.

The Forty-eight Hour Shit:

Where it takes two days for the smell to go away.

The Money Shit:

When you were a kid and you swallowed a dime and your mother had to go through it and it is now in your baby book.

The Cruise Ship Shit:

Where when you flush you have to run and hid under the bed saying, "hit the deck."

The Rubber Glove Shit:

Where you have to go get some rubber gloves to retrieve whatever fell in after you bent over to admire your masterpiece.

The Museum Shit:

Where you swear if you took a picture of such a perfect gem that they would hang it in the Smithsonian.

The Adolph Hitler Shit:

Where you want to go hide in a bunker to get away from it.

The Gandhi Shit:

Where you swear you aren't going to eat another thing as long as you live so nothing so nasty ever comes out again.

The Atom Bomb Shit:

Where it goes down with so much force a mushroom cloud of water sprays your backside.

The In-law Shit:

Where you wish your in-laws were visiting because if they were there they would be sure to leave in a hurry.

The Catfish Shit:

If you leave it at the bottom long enough, it will start to grow whiskers.

The 747 Shit:

It's so big and wide you think you can fit 100 passengers on it.

The Jingle Shit, also know as the Alka Seltzer Shit:

Where you want to sing a jingle like "Plop plop fizz fizz, Oh what a relief it is" while you are doing the deed.

The Eight-Track Tape Shit:

It has been inside of you for so long it is an oldie but goodie.

The Bird Shit, Shit:

When you are one, you are glad you weren't walking under a tree or were reincarnated as a statue.

The Brokeback Mountain Shit:

You are glad it is coming out and not going in.

The Snow Shit:

You never know how much you are going to have or how long it will last.

The Savings Account Shit:

Where you are glad to make a deposit in the porcelain bank.

The Battle of Midway Shit:

Where there are a bunch of floaters and sinkers.

The Masterpiece Shit:

A work of art that even Von Gough would be proud of.

The Princess Shit:

Not too hard, not too soft, but just right.

The Fisherman Shit:

When after you eat a bunch of raw hamburger and you have so many worms coming out of your butt that your buddies want you to open a bait shop.

The Down Under Shit:

When you shit so much you lose 2 whole inches of your "kangaroo pouch" off your stomach.

The Black and Blue Shit:

Where it hurts so much you feel like you just got beat in a title fight.

The Fisherman Shit #2:

When, no matter how many times you flush, there are still a couple of bobbers floating at the surface.

The Third Fisherman Shit:

Where the story of just how big his turd is keeps getting larger.

The Memory Lane Shit:

When the smell reminds you of shits from days gone by.

The Game Show Shit:

Not sure if you are in double jeopardy or final jeopardy.

The Bruce Willis Shit:

Where your ass feels like a scene from a Die Hard movie.

The Rocky Shit:

When you feel like calling out, "Yo Adrian."

The Show and Tell Shit:

Where you want to call up your whole kindergarten class from 30 years ago including the teacher because you finally have something to show them.

The Baby Wipes Shit:

No matter how much toilet paper you use, if you use one of your baby's wipes, you will find out you didn't really get yourself clean.

The Super Bowl Shit:

Where you feel like you should have a large party at your house to celebrate.

The World Series Shit:

Where it felt like it took all seven games but the victory was worth it.

The Albert Einstein Shit:

Where you sat so long you feel like you could have come up with the meaning of MCsquared if he hadn't already done it.

The Valentine Day Shit:

Where it came out shaped like a heart and you want to write be mine on it and call your girlfriend.

The Columbus Day Shit:

Where you feel like the Nina, Pinta, and the Santa Maria all came out.

The Thanksgiving Day Shit:

Where you are very thankful you took a large dump so you had some more room to eat another plate full.

The Christmas Shit:

Where you are glad you have
the day off so you can recover
from it.

The Christmas Shit #2:

When you head to the bathroom
to do your duty and find that
someone has left you a present
in the toilet.

The Forth of July Shit:

Where your ass feels like a roman candle was stuck in there and you are glad it exploded.

The Halloween Shit:

It was so scary that it even scared you.

The Labor Day Shit:

Where you felt like you were in labor for a week and a half.

The Proposal Shit:

Where you get the bright idea to swallow the engagement ring so you can surprise her when you propose, but it backfires when you bring your fiancé into the bathroom to show her your dirty deed and she leaves you before you can find the ring and pop the question.

The Hunger Shit:

When you have to shit so bad you can "taste it."

The Mirror Shit:

Where after you get it out, you stare at it like a teenage girl looks at herself in the mirror.

The $200 Shit:

Where you stop the toilet up so bad you have to call a plumber.

The General George S. Patton Shit:

Where you feel like you have enough shit to start a war.

The General Macarthur Shit:

Where you vow to never return because you stunk up the bathroom so bad.

The Napoleon Shit:

When after you are done your surely know what Napoleon felt like after Waterloo.

The Genghis Kahn Shit:

After you are finished you feel like to have just sacked and razed a whole continent.

The Daylight Savings Shit:

When it is daylight when you sit down, nighttime when you get up and you feel like you lost an hour of your life.

The French Whore Shit:

Where the smell lingers for 3 days.

The Cranberries Shit:

Where the smell "lingers" and you keep singing the song.

The Beetles Shit:

Where it hurts so much you understand what the song Yesterday was all about.

The Gay Man Shit:

When you feel like not only has a hamster crawled up there, it has crawled up there and died.

The Movie Theater Shit:

Where it comes out of your butt like a popcorn maker.

The Sex Toy Shit:

Where you feel like a whole string of Chinese anal love beads are coming out one at a time.

The Duct Tape Shit:

Where when you wipe, the toilet paper sticks to your ass like duct tape because it is so messy.

The Popeye Shit:

Where you wish you would have drank some olive oil to make it come out easier because it feels like it is as big as Bluto.

The Academy Award Shit:

After is finally comes out you start to hear the theme song from Chariots Of Fire.

The Septic Tank Shit:

Where even the guys who come to clean out your septic tank won't come near the bathroom after you are done.

The Air Freshener Shit:

Where it takes a whole can to mask the smell.

The Emergency Room Shit:

Where you feel lucky to make it out of there alive.

The Upper Decker Shit:

Where you take a dump not in the toilet bowl but in the supply tank and laugh so much you get a nosebleed.

The Lone Ranger Shit:

Where you work so hard making what you think is a skyscraper and peer into the toilet when you are done and all you see is one small turd floating there.

The Bus Stop Shit:

When it plops so much it gets your whole butt wet, just like a car hitting a puddle while you are standing at a bus stop.

The 24 Shit:

Where at any moment you feel like Jack Baur is going to break down the bathroom door thinking you are hatching a terrorist plot.

The Survivor Shit:

When you are the last one in the house after they all left from the smell of your dirty deed.

The America's Got Talent Shit:

Where you know if you could have dropped trou on the stage in front of Howie and friends and plopped out such a masterpiece, there was no way you would have been voted off.

The Aircraft Carrier Shit:

A floater that is so big that you know the Navy is going to try to land 3 jets on it.

The Sex Toy Shit:

Where you swear if your kinky old college girlfriend saw it, she would want to use it as a dildo.

The Toilet Bowl Brush Shit:

When you need a toilet bowl brush to clean the sides, the seat and everywhere else after you are finished.

The Inheritance Shit:

When you look in the toilet after you are done and realize that is exactly what you are getting from your parents, and giving to your kids.

The Gay Mans Shit Number 2:

When the first thing that comes out is a dead hamster from last nights sex play.

The religious shit:

When your roommate or spouse blesses it by an exclamation, "Holy shit!" when they barge in and take a whiff.

The Subway shit:

Where it is a foot long,

Made in the USA
Middletown, DE
06 March 2020